Prayer Companion To

שָׁלוֹם עִבְרִית

3

Peri Sinclair

Behrman House Publishers
www.behrmanhouse.com

Book and Cover Design: Itzhack Shelomi
Project Editor: Terry S. Kaye

Table of Contents

אֵין כָּמוֹךָ, אַב הָרַחֲמִים   chapter 1

Soon you will be celebrating your Bar or Bat Mitzvah. You will sit in the
synagogue surrounded by family and friends. You are likely to lead prayers and
read from the Torah. You may be the one to take the Torah from the Ark. Right
before you do, the congregation will join you in chanting two prayers—
אֵין כָּמוֹךָ and אַב הָרַחֲמִים.

Practice reading אֵין כָּמוֹךָ and אַב הָרַחֲמִים aloud.

1. אֵין כָּמוֹךָ בָאֱלֹהִים, יְיָ, וְאֵין כְּמַעֲשֶׂיךָ.

2. מַלְכוּתְךָ מַלְכוּת כָּל עוֹלָמִים וּמֶמְשַׁלְתְּךָ בְּכָל דּוֹר וָדֹר.

3. יְיָ מֶלֶךְ, יְיָ מָלָךְ, יְיָ יִמְלֹךְ לְעוֹלָם וָעֶד.

4. יְיָ עֹז לְעַמּוֹ יִתֵּן, יְיָ יְבָרֵךְ אֶת עַמּוֹ בַשָּׁלוֹם.

5. אַב הָרַחֲמִים, הֵיטִיבָה בִרְצוֹנְךָ אֶת צִיּוֹן,

6. תִּבְנֶה חוֹמוֹת יְרוּשָׁלָיִם.

7. כִּי בְךָ לְבַד בָּטָחְנוּ, מֶלֶךְ אֵל רָם וְנִשָּׂא, אֲדוֹן עוֹלָמִים.

1. *There is none like You, Adonai, among the gods (other nations worship), and there
   are no deeds like Yours.*
2. *Your sovereignty is an eternal sovereignty, and Your reign is from generation to generation.*
3. *Adonai is Ruler, Adonai ruled, Adonai will rule forever and ever.*
4. *May Adonai give strength to people, may Adonai bless the people with peace.*
5. *Merciful Parent, favor Zion with Your goodness,*
6. *rebuild the walls of Jerusalem.*
7. *For in You alone do we trust, sovereign God, high and exalted, eternal Ruler.*

Words built on the root מלכ have "rule" as part of their meaning.
Circle all the words built on the root מלכ in the prayers above.
How many words did you circle? _____

4

Create a Prayer Dictionary

Write the English words or phrases from the list below next to the matching Hebrew.

- LIKE YOUR DEEDS   • WILL RULE   • MERCIFUL (THE MERCY)
- THERE IS/ARE NONE   • LIKE YOU   • SOVEREIGNTY   • WE TRUST

_____	יִמְלֹךְ .5	*there is/are none* אֵין .1
_____	בָּטָחְנוּ .6	_____ כָּמוֹךָ .2
_____	מַלְכוּת .7	_____ הָרַחֲמִים .3
		_____ כְּמַעֲשֶׂיךָ .4

Think About It!

Look back at the words you circled on page 4.

Write the root on which these words are built. _____ _____ _____

What is the English meaning of the root? _____

Why do you think the prayers contain so many words built on this root?

_____

_____

Why do you think the Torah service begins with a prayer praising God and not the Torah?

_____

_____

5

What's Missing?

Complete the lines from אֵין כָּמוֹךָ using the words below.

> • LIKE YOUR DEEDS • LIKE YOU • YOUR SOVEREIGNTY

1. אֵין כָּמוֹךָ בָאֱלֹהִים, יְיָ

1. There is none _____, Adonai, among the gods (other nations worship)

2. וְאֵין כְּמַעֲשֶׂיךָ

2. and none are _____

3. מַלְכוּתְךָ מַלְכוּת כָּל עוֹלָמִים

3. _____ is an eternal sovereignty

What is the common word ending in the underlined Hebrew words above? _____

Look at the English meaning of each word. What does the word ending in each mean?

_____

Word Wise

The word בָּטְחְנוּ is built on the Hebrew root בטח ("trust"). In modern Hebrew—the language people speak in Israel—בִּטָחוֹן is the word for "security."

Circle the three root letters in the word בִּטָחוֹן.

6

Siddur Connections

Read the third line of אֵין כָּמוֹךָ **again below. Underline the words built on the root** מלכ. **How many words did you underline? _____**

יְיָ מֶלֶךְ, יְיָ מָלָךְ, יְיָ יִמְלֹךְ לְעוֹלָם וָעֶד

The following verses all appear in the siddur. Each one has at least one word built on the root מלכ. Circle the word(s) with the root מלכ in each line.

1. כַּכָּתוּב בְּתוֹרָתֶךָ, יְיָ יִמְלֹךְ לְעֹלָם וָעֶד

2. יְיָ מָלָךְ תָּגֵל הָאָרֶץ

3. מַלְכוּתְךָ מַלְכוּת כָּל עוֹלָמִים וּמֶמְשַׁלְתְּךָ בְּכָל דּוֹר וָדֹר

Understanding the Prayer

In אַב הָרַחֲמִים we refer to God as "merciful Parent" or "compassionate Parent." (אָב literally means "father.") We have other names for God built on the root רחמ ("mercy" or "compassion"). They are:

God full of mercy	אֵל מָלֵא רַחֲמִים
the Merciful One	הָרַחֲמָן
compassionate and gracious God	אֵל רַחוּם וְחַנּוּן

At the end of the אַב הָרַחֲמִים prayer we declare our trust in God:

כִּי בְךָ לְבַד בָּטָחְנוּ

Why do you think אַב הָרַחֲמִים **says God is a "compassionate Parent" whom we can trust?**

_____

_____

_____

The Torah Reading

The Torah reading is the highlight of the Shabbat morning service. Each week we read the Torah portion—פָּרָשַׁת הַשָּׁבוּעַ ("portion of the week"). Some congregations also read from the Torah on Monday and Thursday mornings, and on Shabbat afternoons, while other congregations read from the Torah on Friday evenings. The Torah is also read on certain Jewish holidays.

Usually the Bar or Bat Mitzvah reads part of the Torah portion on Shabbat.

When will *you* become a Bar or Bat Mitzvah? _____

Do you know the name of your Torah portion? If so, write it here: _____

Arlo - read. Do. ✓

Did You Know?

The rabbis used the first and last words of the Torah to teach us a lesson. The last word in Deuteronomy—the final book of the Torah—is יִשְׂרָאֵל. The first word in Genesis—the first book in the Torah—is בְּרֵאשִׁית. The last letter in the Torah (ל) and the first letter (ב) together spell the word לֵב ("heart"). The rabbis taught that the Torah is the לֵב of the Jewish people.

Why do you think the rabbis called the Torah the heart of the Jewish people?

_____

_____

Bonus question:

What is the name of the Jewish holiday on which we finish the cycle of Torah readings and begin all over again?

_____

Arlo.

Back to the Sources

Read this excerpt from a midrash (a rabbinic story about the Bible). Then answer the questions that follow.

God's "voice" that proclaimed the Ten Commandments at Mount Sinai was heard by every person at his or her own level, so that each one understood the commandments. Even the youngest children could understand what was being said.   (SHMOT RABA 5:16)

Describe in your own words what this midrash teaches about God's voice on Mount Sinai.

_____

_____

If we generalize from this midrash about the Ten Commandments and include the entire Torah, what special quality does the Torah have?

_____

_____

When you become a Bar or Bat Mitzvah, you will learn how to lead services and read from the Torah. You may even practice taking the Torah out of the Ark. When you do, you will be holding the Jewish people's most precious possession. You'll probably hold it very tight!

The congregation stands when the Torah is taken from the Ark; then members sing prayers of praise to God as they watch the Torah being carried to the *bimah* in a ceremonial circuit through the sanctuary. We call this circuit a *hakafah*.

Practice reading the prayers we say when we take the Torah from the Ark.

1. כִּי מִצִּיּוֹן תֵּצֵא תוֹרָה, וּדְבַר יְיָ מִירוּשָׁלָיִם.

2. בָּרוּךְ שֶׁנָּתַן תּוֹרָה לְעַמּוֹ יִשְׂרָאֵל בִּקְדֻשָּׁתוֹ.

3. לְךָ, יְיָ, הַגְּדֻלָּה וְהַגְּבוּרָה וְהַתִּפְאֶרֶת וְהַנֵּצַח וְהַהוֹד,

4. כִּי כֹל בַּשָּׁמַיִם וּבָאָרֶץ.

5. לְךָ יְיָ הַמַּמְלָכָה וְהַמִּתְנַשֵּׂא לְכֹל לְרֹאשׁ.

1. *For out of Zion shall go forth Torah, and the word of Adonai from Jerusalem.*
2. *Praised is the One, who in holiness gave the Torah to God's people Israel.*

3. *Yours, Adonai, is the greatness and the power and the glory, and the victory, and the majesty,*
4. *for all that is in heaven and on earth is Yours.*
5. *Yours is the sovereignty, Adonai; You are supreme over all.*

Create a Prayer Dictionary

Write the English words or phrases from the list below next to the matching Hebrew.

FROM JERUSALEM   THE GREATNESS   OUT OF ZION   IN HEAVEN

AND ON EARTH   AND THE POWER   IN (GOD'S) HOLINESS

AND THE WORD OF

5. הַגְּדֻלָּה _the Greatness_

6. וְהַגְּבוּרָה _and the power_

7. בַּשָּׁמַיִם _in heaven_

8. וּבָאָרֶץ _and on earth_

1. מִצִּיּוֹן _out of Zion_

2. וּדְבַר _and the word of_

3. מִירוּשָׁלָיִם _from Jerusalem_

4. בִּקְדֻשָׁתוֹ _in (God's) Holiness_

Complete the Prayer

For each pair of underlined Hebrew words in כִּי מִצִּיּוֹן below, only one word belongs in the prayer. Circle the word.

כִּי מִצִּיּוֹן/מִירוּשָׁלָיִם תֵּצֵא הַגְּדֻלָה/תּוֹרָה,

For   out of Zion   shall go forth   Torah

וּבָאָרֶץ/וּדְבַר יְיָ מִירוּשָׁלָיִם/מִצִּיּוֹן.

and the word of   Adonai   from Jerusalem

בָּרוּךְ שֶׁנָּתַן/בִּקְדֻשָׁתוֹ תּוֹרָה לְעַמּוֹ יִשְׂרָאֵל בִּקְדֻשָׁתוֹ/בַּשָּׁמַיִם.

Praised is   who gave   Torah   to God's people   in (God's) holiness
the One   Israel

Did You Know?

Zion is another name for Jerusalem.

Understanding the Prayer

Read the following phrases from לְךָ יְיָ, then complete the activities below.

Yours, Adonai, is the greatness and the power	1. לְךָ, יְיָ, הַגְּדֻלָּה וְהַגְּבוּרָה
and the glory, and the victory, and the majesty,	2. וְהַתִּפְאֶרֶת וְהַנֵּצַח וְהַהוֹד,
for all that is in heaven and on earth is Yours.	3. כִּי כֹל בַּשָּׁמַיִם וּבָאָרֶץ.

- Draw a square around the Hebrew word that means "the greatness."
- Underline the Hebrew word that means "and the power."
- Draw a squiggly line under the Hebrew word that means "in heaven."
- Circle the Hebrew word that means "and on earth."

Why do you think we sing this prayer as the Torah is taken out of the Ark and paraded through the sanctuary?

_____

_____

Think About It!

You'd expect a king or queen to wear a crown, wouldn't you? But thousands of years ago, when the Jews were ruled by kings, the kings were not "crowned," but rather were anointed with oil in a religious ceremony. A priest would pour oil over the head of the new ruler of Israel and declare the person king. Even though kings were not crowned, we have always placed a crown on the Torah!

Suggest one reason that the Torah wears a crown while Jewish kings did not.

_____

Did you know that in the United Kingdom, people bow towards the Torah as it is carried past them, as they would towards the Queen of England?

What customs does your congregation have to honor the Torah?

_____

_____

Prayer Arithmetic

The following pairs of equations will help you discover two basic rules in Hebrew grammar. For the first pair, read both sets of words. Subtract the words on the second line from the words on the first and write your answer on the blank below. Repeat with the second pair of equations. The pair in each equation should have the same solution.

from Jerusalem = מִירוּשָׁלַיִם

  – Jerusalem = יְרוּשָׁלַיִם

_____

_____ = מְ

out of (from) Zion = מִצִּיוֹן   **1**

  – Zion = צִיּוֹן

_____

_____ = מְ

and the power = וְהַגְּבוּרָה

  – the power = הַגְּבוּרָה

_____

_____ = וְ

and the word of = וּדְבַר   **2**

  – the word of = דְּבַר

_____

_____ = וּ

1. What does the prefix מְ mean? _____

2. What do the prefixes וּ and וְ mean? _____

Turn back to the prayers on page 10. Circle all the forms of the וְ prefix. How many prefixes did you circle? _____

13

Holding the Torah

In many congregations, the person holding the Torah after it is taken out of the Ark recites the following lines, first alone, and then with the congregation. In other congregations, all the worshipers say the lines together.

1. שְׁמַע יִשְׂרָאֵל: יְיָ אֱלֹהֵינוּ, יְיָ אֶחָד.

2. אֶחָד אֱלֹהֵינוּ, גָּדוֹל אֲדוֹנֵינוּ, קָדוֹשׁ שְׁמוֹ.

1. Hear O Israel: Adonai is our God, Adonai is One.

2. Our God is One and is great; God's name is holy.

In some congregations a third line is added. The person holding the Torah turns to face the Ark and bows while reciting this line.

3. גַּדְּלוּ לַיְיָ אִתִּי, וּנְרוֹמְמָה שְׁמוֹ יַחְדָּו.

3. Make Adonai great with me, and together let us exalt God's name.

Why do you think we say the Sh'ma when we take the Torah out of the Ark?

_____

_____

Back to the Sources

Read the following excerpt from the Mishnah (rabbinic commentary on the Torah). Then answer the questions that follow.

> Rabbi Elazar ben Azaryah said: Where there is no Torah there is no *derech eretz* (the right way to behave); and where there is no *derech eretz* there is no Torah….
>
> He used to say: A person whose wisdom is greater than his or her deeds is like a tree whose branches are many but whose roots are few. Such a tree can easily be uprooted by a strong wind. However, a person who does many good deeds but is not as wise is like a tree whose branches are few but whose roots are many; even the strongest wind in the world can blow and blow and still would not be able to uproot it.
>
> (AVOT 3:17)

Describe in your own words what the terms "Torah" and "*derech eretz*" represent.

Torah _____

Derech eretz _____

Do you think comparing a person to a tree is effective in the rabbi's quote? Why or why not?

_____

_____

_____

Every *parashah*—Torah portion—is divided into sections, or readings. For each section, one or more congregants are called up to the Torah to say two blessings—one blessing before the Torah reader begins to read that section, and one after the reader has finished. Coming up to the Torah to recite these blessings is known as an עֲלִיָּה. A high point of *your* Bar or Bat Mitzvah ceremony will be the moment when you are called up for an עֲלִיָּה to the Torah.

Practice reading aloud the blessings before and after the Torah reading.

Before the Torah reading

1. *Praise Adonai, who is praised.*   1. בָּרְכוּ אֶת יְיָ הַמְבֹרָךְ.

   2. בָּרוּךְ יְיָ הַמְבֹרָךְ לְעוֹלָם וָעֶד.

2. *Praised is Adonai, who is praised forever and ever.*

   3. בָּרוּךְ אַתָּה, יְיָ אֱלֹהֵינוּ, מֶלֶךְ הָעוֹלָם,

3. *Praised are You, Adonai our God, Ruler of the world,*

4. *who chose us from all the nations*   4. אֲשֶׁר בָּחַר בָּנוּ מִכָּל הָעַמִּים

5. *and gave us God's Torah.*   5. וְנָתַן לָנוּ אֶת תּוֹרָתוֹ.

6. *Praised are You, Adonai, who gives us the Torah.*   6. בָּרוּךְ אַתָּה, יְיָ, נוֹתֵן הַתּוֹרָה.

After the Torah reading

   3. בָּרוּךְ אַתָּה, יְיָ אֱלֹהֵינוּ, מֶלֶךְ הָעוֹלָם,

3. *Praised are You, Adonai our God, Ruler of the world,*

4. *who gave us the Torah of truth,*   4. אֲשֶׁר נָתַן לָנוּ תּוֹרַת אֱמֶת,

5. *and implanted within us eternal life.*   5. וְחַיֵּי עוֹלָם נָטַע בְּתוֹכֵנוּ.

6. *Praised are You, Adonai, who gives us the Torah.*   6. בָּרוּךְ אַתָּה, יְיָ, נוֹתֵן הַתּוֹרָה.

Challenge

Underline the lines that appear in both blessings.

Create a Prayer Dictionary

Write the English words or phrases from the list below next to the matching Hebrew.

· THE TORAH OF TRUTH ✓ · AND ETERNAL LIFE ✓ · GAVE ✓ · GIVES ✓
· THE NATIONS ✓ · US ✓ · FROM ALL ✓ · CHOSE ✓

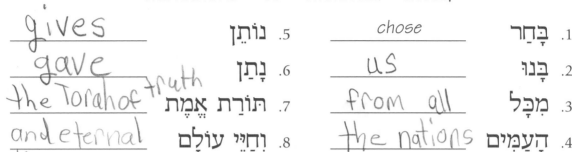

gives _____ נוֹתֵן .5

gave _____ נָתַן .6

the Torah of truth תּוֹרַת אֱמֶת .7

and eternal life וְחַיֵּי עוֹלָם .8

chose _____ בָּחַר .1

us _____ בָּנוּ .2

from all _____ מִכָּל .3

the nations הָעַמִּים .4

Prayer Building Blocks

In the blessing before the Torah reading, we thank God for choosing us to receive the Torah and for giving us the Torah. In the blessing after the reading, we thank God again for giving us the Torah of truth and for granting us eternal life.

What sorts of responsibilities do you think come with receiving the Torah?

I think some responsibilities are not to lie.

How do you think the Torah gives the Jewish people "eternal life"?

_____

_____

_____

H~W
10-19

Crossword

Read the Hebrew clues and fill in the correct English words from the Torah blessings.

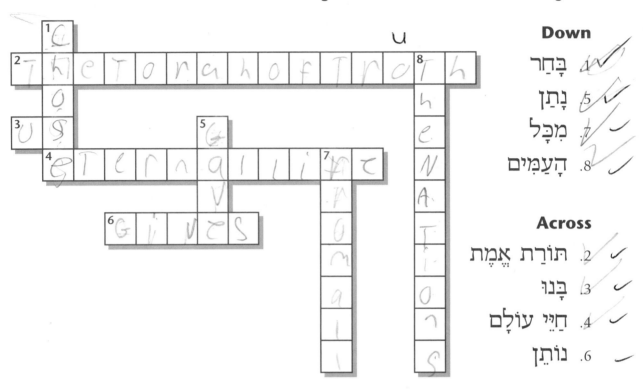

Crossword answers filled in:
- 1 Down: C O U S
- 2 Across: The Torah of Truth
- 3 Across: US
- 4 Across: Eternal life
- 5 Down: G V
- 6 Across: Gives
- 8 Down: The Nations

Down

בָּחַר .1

נָתַן .5

מִכָּל .7

הָעַמִּים .8

Across

תּוֹרַת אֱמֶת .2

בָּנוּ .3

חַיֵּי עוֹלָם .4

נוֹתֵן .6

Think About It!

We have learned that the honor of being called up to the *bimah* to recite the blessings before and after the sections in the Torah reading is called an עֲלִיָה, which literally means "going up" or "ascending." Did you know that going to live in Israel is called "making עֲלִיָה"?

Why do you think we "go up" or "ascend" to the Torah?

_____

_____

Why do you think we "go up" or "ascend" to live in Israel?

_____

_____

18

The Torah Reading

It is not easy to read from the Torah. You must be trained to read Hebrew without vowels or punctuation. What's more, in most synagogues the Torah portion is chanted using special musical inflections or melodies called "trope." That's why the community appoints Torah readers with this special knowledge to do the actual reading.

The Torah reader often practices in a *tikkun*, a book in which each Torah portion is laid out in two parallel columns; one column is in regular block Hebrew letters with vowels and trope signs, and the other column is as it would appear in a Torah scroll.

Do you recognize the word *tikkun* from the phrase *tikkun olam* ("fixing the world" or "repairing the world")? The *tikkun* in which we prepare to read Torah "fixes" or "repairs" our mistakes.

בראשית

בְּרֵאשִׁית בָּרָא אֱלֹהִים אֵת הַשָּׁמַיִם וְאֵת הָאָרֶץ: וְהָאָרֶץ א 2
הָיְתָה תֹהוּ וָבֹהוּ וְחֹשֶׁךְ עַל־פְּנֵי תְהוֹם וְרוּחַ אֱלֹהִים
מְרַחֶפֶת עַל־פְּנֵי הַמָּיִם: וַיֹּאמֶר אֱלֹהִים יְהִי אוֹר וַיְהִי־ 3
אוֹר: וַיַּרְא אֱלֹהִים אֶת־הָאוֹר כִּי־טוֹב וַיַּבְדֵּל אֱלֹהִים בֵּין 4
הָאוֹר וּבֵין הַחֹשֶׁךְ: וַיִּקְרָא אֱלֹהִים לָאוֹר יוֹם וְלַחֹשֶׁךְ ה
קָרָא לָיְלָה וַיְהִי־עֶרֶב וַיְהִי־בֹקֶר יוֹם אֶחָד: פ ·שׁ·

Connect each Torah letter below to the matching printed letter.

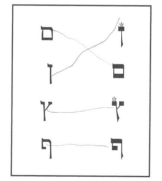

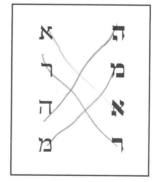

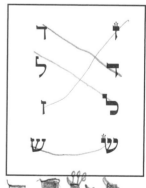

Write your Hebrew name in Torah letters. _____

Did you know that the שְׁמַע comes from the Torah? If you were to open a Torah scroll to Deuteronomy Chapter 6, Verse 4, you'd spot this very familiar prayer.

Look at the שְׁמַע as it appears in the Torah. In what way is it different from the other lines in the Torah?

שְׁמַע ישראל יהוה אלהינו יהוה אחד

_____

_____

If you take the two enlarged letters and put them together backwards and forwards, they spell two Hebrew words: עֵד ("witness") and דַע ("know"). The rabbis teach that each of us should both *be a witness* and *know* that there is only one God. Once we know that there is one God, we can be a witness to that fact.

Explain in your own words what a witness does.

a witness is someone who witnesses somthing / sees something

Lifting and Dressing the Torah
הַגְבָּהָה וּגְלִילָה

At the end of the Torah reading, two more people are called up to the *bimah*:

(1) the מַגְבִּיהַ (man) or מַגְבִּיהָה (woman), the person who lifts the Torah

(2) the גּוֹלֵל (man) or גּוֹלֶלֶת (woman), who rolls the Torah, then dresses it.

Many congregations sing the following words as the Torah is lifted:

וְזֹאת הַתּוֹרָה אֲשֶׁר שָׂם מֹשֶׁה לִפְנֵי בְּנֵי יִשְׂרָאֵל, עַל פִּי יְיָ
בְּיַד מֹשֶׁה.

This is the Torah that Moses placed before the people of Israel, by the word of Adonai through Moses.

In some congregations, when the מַגְבִּיהָה or מַגְבִּיהַ holds up the Torah, the members lift their pinky fingers or the fringes of their *tallitot* and hold them toward the Torah as if pointing to the section read. Then the גּוֹלֵל or גּוֹלֶלֶת ties the Torah and dresses it with its mantle and ornaments.

Why do you think we raise the Torah for the entire congregation to see?

_____

_____

_____

The תַּנַ"ךְ (Bible) is divided into three parts. The תּוֹרָה (Torah) is the first part; נְבִיאִים (Prophets) is second; and כְּתוּבִים (Writings), which includes psalms and proverbs, is third. After the Torah reading on Shabbat and holidays, an honored person—that could be *you* on your Bar or Bat Mitzvah!—is usually called up to read a section from the Book of Prophets called the הַפְטָרָה. The הַפְטָרָה is often connected by theme to the weekly פָּרָשָׁה.

We say a blessing before chanting the הַפְטָרָה. Practice reading the blessing aloud.

1. בָּרוּךְ אַתָּה, יְיָ אֱלֹהֵינוּ, מֶלֶךְ הָעוֹלָם,

2. אֲשֶׁר בָּחַר בִּנְבִיאִים טוֹבִים,

3. וְרָצָה בְדִבְרֵיהֶם הַנֶּאֱמָרִים בֶּאֱמֶת.

4. בָּרוּךְ אַתָּה יְיָ, הַבּוֹחֵר בַּתּוֹרָה וּבְמֹשֶׁה עַבְדּוֹ,

5. וּבְיִשְׂרָאֵל עַמּוֹ, וּבִנְבִיאֵי הָאֱמֶת וָצֶדֶק.

1. Praised are You, Adonai our God, Ruler of the world,
2. who chose good (faithful) prophets,
3. and was pleased with their words spoken in truth.
4. Praised are You, Adonai, who takes delight in (chooses) the Torah, and in Moses, God's servant,
5. and in Israel, God's people, and in prophets of truth and justice.

Explain in your own words how the prophets—נְבִיאִים—are described in the blessing.

_____

_____

Create a Prayer Dictionary

Write the English words or phrases from the list below next to the matching Hebrew.

• IN TRUTH • CHOSE • IN PROPHETS • AND JUSTICE • GOOD (FAITHFUL)

4. בֶּאֱמֶת _____

1. בָּחַר _____ chose _____

5. וְצֶדֶק _____

2. בִּנְבִיאִים _____

3. טוֹבִים _____

The Family Connection

There are three sets of related words in the blessing before the הַפְטָרָה reading.
Connect each pair of related words.

הָאֱמֶת   1. בָּחַר

הַבּוֹחֵר   2. בִּנְבִיאִים

וּבִנְבִיאֵי   3. בֶּאֱמֶת

Now write one of the words from each pair next to the English meaning.

1. prophets _____

2. choose _____

3. truth _____

It's Good!

Do you know the word טוֹב ("good")? Find and circle the letters טוֹב in the following word: טוֹבִים.

In what way were the prophets "good"? _____

_____

Psalm 15 teaches us the importance of telling the truth (אֱמֶת). Read the excerpt below, then answer the questions that follow.

מִזְמוֹר לְדָוִד: יְיָ מִי־יָגוּר בְּאָהֳלֶךָ מִי־יִשְׁכֹּן בְּהַר קָדְשֶׁךָ.

...וְדֹבֵר אֱמֶת בִּלְבָבוֹ. לֹא־רָגַל עַל־לְשֹׁנוֹ...

A psalm of David: Adonai, who will dwell in Your tent? Who will live on Your holy mountain? Those who … speak truth in their hearts , and have no slander on their tongue …

Write the word "truth" in Hebrew. _____

In the blessing before the הַפְטָרָה, **the prophets are called** נְבִיאֵי הָאֱמֶת וָצֶדֶק ("prophets of truth and justice"). **Describe one way you can be a "prophet of truth and justice" in your own circle of friends, your school, or your community.**

_____

In addition to being truthful to others, why is it important to be truthful to ourselves?

_____

The Maftir and Maftirah

The last person called to the Torah on Shabbat is known as the *maftir* (man or boy) or the *maftirah* (woman or girl). This is often the Bar Mitzvah or Bat Mitzvah. The *maftir* or *maftirah* recites the blessings before and after the reading of the last few verses of the Torah portion, and then chants the haftarah. Can you see the connection between the words *maftir* and *maftirah* and haftarah?

Both the Torah and the haftarah are chanted according to musical inflections (trope), but the tunes of the trope for the Torah and haftarah are different. While the Torah is chanted from a scroll that is rolled from one portion to the next, the haftarah is chanted from a printed book.

The Blessings after the Haftarah

You have learned about the blessing *before* the haftarah reading. We also say four blessings *after* the haftarah reading. The first three have to do with promises made by God to the Jewish people. The fourth and final blessing thanks God for the Torah, the worship service, the prophets, and Shabbat.

Practice reading aloud the four blessings after the haftarah reading.

I

1. בָּרוּךְ אַתָּה, יְיָ אֱלֹהֵינוּ, מֶלֶךְ הָעוֹלָם, צוּר כָּל הָעוֹלָמִים, צַדִּיק

2. בְּכָל הַדּוֹרוֹת, הָאֵל הַנֶּאֱמָן, הָאוֹמֵר וְעוֹשֶׂה, הַמְדַבֵּר

3. וּמְקַיֵּם, שֶׁכָּל־דְּבָרָיו אֱמֶת וָצֶדֶק.

4. נֶאֱמָן אַתָּה הוּא, יְיָ אֱלֹהֵינוּ, וְנֶאֱמָנִים דְּבָרֶיךָ, וְדָבָר אֶחָד

5. מִדְּבָרֶיךָ, אָחוֹר לֹא יָשׁוּב רֵיקָם, כִּי אֵל מֶלֶךְ נֶאֱמָן וְרַחֲמָן אָתָּה.

6. בָּרוּךְ אַתָּה, יְיָ, הָאֵל הַנֶּאֱמָן בְּכָל־דְּבָרָיו.

II

7. רַחֵם עַל־צִיּוֹן כִּי הִיא בֵּית חַיֵּינוּ, וְלַעֲלוּבַת נֶפֶשׁ תּוֹשִׁיעַ

8. בִּמְהֵרָה בְיָמֵינוּ. בָּרוּךְ אַתָּה, יְיָ, מְשַׂמֵּחַ צִיּוֹן בְּבָנֶיהָ.

III

9. שַׂמְּחֵנוּ, יְיָ אֱלֹהֵינוּ, בְּאֵלִיָּהוּ הַנָּבִיא עַבְדֶּךָ וּבְמַלְכוּת בֵּית דָּוִד

10. מְשִׁיחֶךָ, בִּמְהֵרָה יָבֹא וְיָגֵל לִבֵּנוּ. עַל־כִּסְאוֹ לֹא־יֵשֶׁב זָר

11. וְלֹא־יִנְחֲלוּ עוֹד אֲחֵרִים אֶת כְּבוֹדוֹ, כִּי בְּשֵׁם קָדְשְׁךָ נִשְׁבַּעְתָּ

12. לוֹ שֶׁלֹּא־יִכְבֶּה נֵרוֹ לְעוֹלָם וָעֶד. בָּרוּךְ אַתָּה, יְיָ, מָגֵן דָּוִד.

IV

13. עַל־הַתּוֹרָה, וְעַל־הָעֲבוֹדָה, וְעַל הַנְּבִיאִים, וְעַל־יוֹם הַשַּׁבָּת הַזֶּה,

14. שֶׁנָּתַתָּ־לָּנוּ, יְיָ אֱלֹהֵינוּ, לִקְדֻשָּׁה וְלִמְנוּחָה, לְכָבוֹד וּלְתִפְאָרֶת,

15. עַל־הַכֹּל, יְיָ אֱלֹהֵינוּ, אֲנַחְנוּ מוֹדִים לָךְ, וּמְבָרְכִים אוֹתָךְ.

16. יִתְבָּרַךְ שִׁמְךָ בְּפִי כָּל־חַי תָּמִיד לְעוֹלָם וָעֶד.

17. בָּרוּךְ אַתָּה, יְיָ, מְקַדֵּשׁ הַשַּׁבָּת.

Words from the Prophets

The prophets, whose words we read in the haftarah, taught the Jewish people how to behave according to God's laws.

Read the following excerpts from the Book of Prophets.

מִשְׁפַּט אֱמֶת שְׁפֹטוּ וְחֶסֶד וְרַחֲמִים עֲשׂוּ אִישׁ אֶת־אָחִיו:...

...practice true judgment; deal loyally and compassionately with one another.

(ZECHARIAH 7:9)

גֵּר יָתוֹם וְאַלְמָנָה לֹא תַעֲשֹׁקוּ וְדָם נָקִי אַל־תִּשְׁפְּכוּ...

Do not oppress the stranger, the orphan, or the widow; and do not shed innocent blood....

(JEREMIAH 7:6)

וּמָה יְיָ דּוֹרֵשׁ מִמְּךָ כִּי אִם־עֲשׂוֹת מִשְׁפָּט וְאַהֲבַת חֶסֶד...

...and what Adonai requires of you: only to do justice and to love goodness.... (MICAH 6:8)

What is the common theme among the prophets? _____

_____

Why do you think they all focused on this theme?

_____

_____

Which of the prophets' words or phrases above do you consider to be most important? Explain your answer.

_____

Giving tzedakah is one way we can behave according to the laws of the Torah. Maimonides—also known as the Rambam, the acronym for Rabbi Moses Ben Maimon—was a great rabbi, author, and philosopher. He defined eight levels—a "ladder"—of tzedakah. At the top of the ladder is the best or most praiseworthy way of giving tzedakah.

Read a description of Maimonides' levels of tzedakah below, then answer the questions that follow.

There are eight different ways of giving tzedakah. The least praiseworthy level is #1 and the most praiseworthy is #8.

1. Giving reluctantly and with regret.
2. Giving graciously, but less than one should.
3. Giving what one should, but only after being asked.
4. Giving before being asked.
5. Giving without knowing the identity of the recipient, although the recipient knows the identity of the giver.
6. Giving anonymously, though the giver knows who the recipient is.
7. Giving without knowing the identity of the recipient, and without the recipient knowing the identity of the giver.
8. Helping the recipient become self-supporting through a gift or a loan, or by finding employment for the recipient.

According to Maimonides, what is the best way to give tzedakah? Give an example of how one can give tzedakah in this way.

_____

Why do you think Maimonides called this the highest level of tzedakah?

_____

Each of Maimonides' eight steps on the tzedakah ladder suggests a different relationship between the giver and the recipient. Do you think these relationships matter? Why or why not?

_____

_____

chapter 5

Just as we take the Torah out of the אֲרוֹן קֹדֶשׁ ("Holy Ark") with songs and praises to God and then a *hakafah* through the sanctuary, so do we return it to the אֲרוֹן קֹדֶשׁ with the same ceremony and celebration. As we get ready to return the Torah to the אֲרוֹן קֹדֶשׁ, we sing יְהַלְלוּ, a song of praise to God.

Practice reading יְהַלְלוּ aloud.

1. יְהַלְלוּ אֶת שֵׁם יְיָ, כִּי נִשְׂגָּב שְׁמוֹ לְבַדּוֹ.

2. הוֹדוֹ עַל אֶרֶץ וְשָׁמָיִם, וַיָּרֶם קֶרֶן לְעַמּוֹ,

3. תְּהִלָּה לְכָל חֲסִידָיו,

4. לִבְנֵי יִשְׂרָאֵל עַם קְרוֹבוֹ.

5. הַלְלוּיָהּ.

1. *Let us give praise to the name of Adonai, for God's name alone is exalted.*

2. *God's splendor is on earth and in the heavens, God gives God's people strength,*

3. *Giving praise to all of God's faithful followers,*

4. *to the children of Israel—a people close to God.*

5. *Halleluyah.*

Read the English translation of יְהַלְלוּ again. Is the way in which we praise God different from the way in which we praise people? Explain your answer.

_____

_____

_____

Create a Prayer Dictionary

Write the English words or phrases from the list below next to the matching Hebrew.

• PEOPLE / NATION   • LET US GIVE PRAISE   • NAME

3. עַם _____   1. יְהַלְלוּ _____

                                 2. שֵׁם _____

Complete the Prayer

Using the Hebrew Prayer Dictionary words above, fill in the blanks in the lines below.

1. _____ אֶת _____ יְיָ, כִּי נִשְׂגָּב שְׁמוֹ לְבַדּוֹ.

2. לִבְנֵי יִשְׂרָאֵל _____ קְרוֹבוֹ.

Get to the Root

The root of יְהַלְלוּ is הלל. Words built on the root הלל have "praise" as part of their meaning.

Write the root of יְהַלְלוּ. _____ _____ _____

Singing songs is one way in which we praise God. What is another way in which we praise God?

_____

Did You Know?

Pesukei DeZimra are psalms of song and praise in the morning prayer service. Thousands of years ago, in the days of the Holy Temple, the Priests chanted songs in the morning, accompanied by music. According to Jewish legend, angels sing in the heavens all day long, but especially in the morning. We act like the angels by singing songs of praise. We hope this will inspire us to behave in other "angelic" ways for the rest of the day!

The אַשְׁרֵי—a compilation of lines from psalms—is a poem of praise to God. We recite the אַשְׁרֵי during the opening morning prayers, in the afternoon מִנְחָה service, and before concluding the Torah service and returning the Torah to the Ark.

Practice reading the אַשְׁרֵי aloud.

1. אַשְׁרֵי יוֹשְׁבֵי בֵיתֶךָ, עוֹד יְהַלְלוּךָ סֶּלָה.

Happy are those who dwell in Your house; they will praise You forever.

2. אַשְׁרֵי הָעָם שֶׁכָּכָה לּוֹ, אַשְׁרֵי הָעָם שֶׁיְיָ אֱלֹהָיו.

Happy are the people who are so favored; happy are the people whose God is Adonai.

3. תְּהִלָּה לְדָוִד,

4. אֲרוֹמִמְךָ אֱלוֹהַי הַמֶּלֶךְ, וַאֲבָרְכָה שִׁמְךָ לְעוֹלָם וָעֶד.

5. בְּכָל יוֹם אֲבָרְכֶךָּ, וַאֲהַלְלָה שִׁמְךָ לְעוֹלָם וָעֶד.

6. גָּדוֹל יְיָ וּמְהֻלָּל מְאֹד, וְלִגְדֻלָּתוֹ אֵין חֵקֶר.

7. דּוֹר לְדוֹר יְשַׁבַּח מַעֲשֶׂיךָ, וּגְבוּרֹתֶיךָ יַגִּידוּ.

8. הֲדַר כְּבוֹד הוֹדֶךָ, וְדִבְרֵי נִפְלְאֹתֶיךָ אָשִׂיחָה.

9. וֶעֱזוּז נוֹרְאֹתֶיךָ יֹאמֵרוּ, וּגְדֻלָּתְךָ אֲסַפְּרֶנָּה.

10. זֵכֶר רַב טוּבְךָ יַבִּיעוּ, וְצִדְקָתְךָ יְרַנֵּנוּ.

11. חַנּוּן וְרַחוּם יְיָ, אֶרֶךְ אַפַּיִם וּגְדָל חָסֶד.

12. טוֹב יְיָ לַכֹּל, וְרַחֲמָיו עַל כָּל מַעֲשָׂיו.

13. יוֹדוּךָ יְיָ כָּל מַעֲשֶׂיךָ, וַחֲסִידֶיךָ יְבָרְכוּכָה.

14. כְּבוֹד מַלְכוּתְךָ יֹאמֵרוּ, וּגְבוּרָתְךָ יְדַבֵּרוּ.

15. לְהוֹדִיעַ לִבְנֵי הָאָדָם גְּבוּרֹתָיו, וּכְבוֹד הֲדַר מַלְכוּתוֹ.

16. מַלְכוּתְךָ מַלְכוּת כָּל עוֹלָמִים, וּמֶמְשַׁלְתְּךָ בְּכָל דּוֹר וָדֹר.

17. סוֹמֵךְ יְיָ לְכָל הַנֹּפְלִים, וְזוֹקֵף לְכָל הַכְּפוּפִים.

18. עֵינֵי כֹל אֵלֶיךָ יְשַׂבֵּרוּ, וְאַתָּה נוֹתֵן לָהֶם אֶת אָכְלָם בְּעִתּוֹ.

19. פּוֹתֵחַ אֶת יָדֶךָ, וּמַשְׂבִּיעַ לְכָל חַי רָצוֹן.

20. צַדִּיק יְיָ בְּכָל דְּרָכָיו, וְחָסִיד בְּכָל מַעֲשָׂיו.

21. קָרוֹב יְיָ לְכָל קֹרְאָיו, לְכֹל אֲשֶׁר יִקְרָאֻהוּ בֶאֱמֶת.

22. רְצוֹן יְרֵאָיו יַעֲשֶׂה, וְאֶת שַׁוְעָתָם יִשְׁמַע וְיוֹשִׁיעֵם.

23. שׁוֹמֵר יְיָ אֶת כָּל אֹהֲבָיו, וְאֵת כָּל הָרְשָׁעִים יַשְׁמִיד.

24. תְּהִלַּת יְיָ יְדַבֶּר פִּי, וִיבָרֵךְ כָּל בָּשָׂר שֵׁם קָדְשׁוֹ לְעוֹלָם וָעֶד.

25. וַאֲנַחְנוּ נְבָרֵךְ יָהּ, מֵעַתָּה וְעַד עוֹלָם. הַלְלוּיָהּ.

And we will praise God, now and forever. Halleluyah!

Read the first two lines of the אַשְׁרֵי again.

What do you think it means to "dwell in God's house"?

_____

_____

The אַשְׁרֵי, like many other *piyyutim* (poetic prayers), is written in an acrostic form. In an acrostic, the initial letters of each line spell out a new word—often the author's name—or they form a pattern.

Circle the first letter on lines 4–24 in the אַשְׁרֵי.

What letter pattern does the אַשְׁרֵי follow? __אלף בית ת__

Which letter is missing from the acrostic? __נ__

Many congregations add the אַשְׁרֵי before putting the Torah back into the Ark.

Write a reason for adding this extra poem of praise.

_____

_____

31

The Jewish People

You have learned that the word עַם means "people" or "nation."

Read the names for the Jewish people below.

Circle the word עַם in each Hebrew name.

the people of Israel	עַם יִשְׂרָאֵל .1
the Jewish people	הָעַם הַיְהוּדִי .2
the people of the Book	עַם הַסֵּפֶר .3
the holy people	עַם קָדוֹשׁ .4
the eternal people	עַם עוֹלָם .5

Choose one of the names above that you like best. Explain your choice.

I like the people of Israel because
I like the song that its
in

In the אַשְׁרֵי, "God's house" probably originally meant the Temple in Jerusalem. Today we can think of other explanations for "God's house." Each of the excerpts below from Pirkei Avot 1:4–5 reflects a different view of the ideal Jewish home. Read the excerpts, then answer the questions that follow.

Yossi Ben Yo'ezer from Tzreida said: Let your home be a gathering place for scholars; may you become dusty in the dust of their feet, and may you drink in their words with thirst.

Yossi ben Yochanan from Jerusalem said: Let your home be open wide to the multitudes. Let the poor be like children in your home….

In your opinion, which of these two models represents "God's house" in the אַשְׁרֵי? Explain your answer.

_____

_____

_____

Can one house include both scholars and the poor? Why or why not?

_____

_____

_____

You have learned that we sing songs of praise to God when we return the Torah to the Ark. One of those songs, Psalm 29, מִזְמוֹר לְדָוִד, describes the power of God's "voice." As you read the English translation of the prayer, be alert to all the metaphors depicting the power of God's voice.

Practice reading Psalm 29 aloud.

1. מִזְמוֹר לְדָוִד,

2. הָבוּ לַיָי, בְּנֵי אֵלִים, הָבוּ לַיָי כָּבוֹד וָעֹז.

3. הָבוּ לַיָי כְּבוֹד שְׁמוֹ, הִשְׁתַּחֲווּ לַיָי בְּהַדְרַת קֹדֶשׁ.

4. קוֹל יְיָ עַל הַמָּיִם, אֵל הַכָּבוֹד הִרְעִים, יְיָ עַל מַיִם רַבִּים.

5. קוֹל יְיָ בַּכֹּחַ, קוֹל יְיָ בֶּהָדָר.

6. קוֹל יְיָ שֹׁבֵר אֲרָזִים, וַיְשַׁבֵּר יְיָ אֶת אַרְזֵי הַלְּבָנוֹן.

7. וַיַּרְקִידֵם כְּמוֹ עֵגֶל, לְבָנוֹן וְשִׂרְיוֹן כְּמוֹ בֶן רְאֵמִים.

8. קוֹל יְיָ חֹצֵב לַהֲבוֹת אֵשׁ.

9. קוֹל יְיָ יָחִיל מִדְבָּר, יָחִיל יְיָ מִדְבַּר קָדֵשׁ.

10. קוֹל יְיָ יְחוֹלֵל אַיָּלוֹת,

11. וַיֶּחֱשֹׂף יְעָרוֹת, וּבְהֵיכָלוֹ כֻּלּוֹ אֹמֵר כָּבוֹד.

12. יְיָ לַמַּבּוּל יָשָׁב, וַיֵּשֶׁב יְיָ מֶלֶךְ לְעוֹלָם.

13. יְיָ עֹז לְעַמּוֹ יִתֵּן, יְיָ יְבָרֵךְ אֶת עַמּוֹ בַשָּׁלוֹם.

1. *A song of David,*
2. *Praise Adonai, all mighty beings, praise Adonai for God's glory and strength.*
3. *Praise Adonai whose name is great, worship Adonai in sacred holiness.*
4. *The voice of Adonai is above the waters, the God of glory echoes over oceans.*

5. *The voice of Adonai is powerful, the voice of Adonai is majestic.*

6. *The voice of Adonai breaks cedar trees, it shatters the cedar trees of Lebanon;*

7. *until the hills of Lebanon skip like rams, and the mountains of Serion like an ox.*

8. *The voice of Adonai sparks fiery flames.*

9. *The voice of Adonai makes the desert shudder, it makes the Kadesh desert tremble.*

10. *The voice of Adonai makes rams dance,*

11. *it uproots forests, while in God's temple all cry "Glory!"*

12. *Adonai ruled over the flood, Adonai will rule forever.*

13. *Adonai will strengthen the people, Adonai will bless God's people with peace.*

List four ways in which the poet describes the power of God's voice.

1. _____

2. _____

3. _____

4. _____

Create a Prayer Dictionary

Write the English words or phrases from the list below next to the matching Hebrew.

• TO/OF DAVID • VOICE • GOD'S PEOPLE • STRENGTH • WITH PEACE

_____ עַמּוֹ .4   *to/of David* לְדָוִד .1

_____ בְּשָׁלוֹם .5   _____ קוֹל .2

_____ עֹז .3

Make a Match

Connect the Hebrew words to the matching English.

voice   לְדָוִד .1

with peace   קוֹל .2

God's people   עֹז .3

strength   עַמּוֹ .4

to/of David   בְּשָׁלוֹם .5

Think About It!

How many times does the word קוֹל ("voice") appear in the psalm? _____

Based on the images in the psalm, how do you think one *hears* the "voice of God"?

_____

_____

A Tree of Life

When we return the Torah to the Ark, we sing עֵץ חַיִּים הִיא, a prayer that compares the Torah to a tree of life. As you read the English translation, think about the qualities of a tree and why the prayer uses that metaphor.

Practice reading עֵץ חַיִּים הִיא aloud.

1. עֵץ חַיִּים הִיא לַמַּחֲזִיקִים בָּהּ, וְתוֹמְכֶיהָ מְאֻשָּׁר.

2. דְּרָכֶיהָ דַרְכֵי נֹעַם, וְכָל נְתִיבוֹתֶיהָ שָׁלוֹם.

3. הֲשִׁיבֵנוּ יְיָ אֵלֶיךָ וְנָשׁוּבָה, חַדֵּשׁ יָמֵינוּ כְּקֶדֶם.

1. *It (the Torah) is a tree of life to those who hold fast to it, and those who support it are happy.*
2. *Its ways are ways of pleasantness, and all its paths are peace.*
3. *Let us return to You, Adonai, and renew our days as they were in the past.*

In what ways is the Torah a "tree of life"?

_____

_____

_____

Interpret It

Now make up your own comparison for the Torah. Complete the sentence below.

The Torah is like a _____ **because** _____

_____

_____ .

Tanach Talk

עֵץ חַיִּים הִיא is taken from the תַּנַ"ךְ (Proverbs 3).

Below is the excerpt from Proverbs in which עֵץ חַיִּים הִיא is found.

Underline all the words of the עֵץ חַיִּים הִיא prayer. Then read the Biblical excerpt.

> 16 אֹרֶךְ יָמִים בִּימִינָהּ
> בִּשְׂמֹאולָהּ עֹשֶׁר וְכָבוֹד:
>
> 17 דְּרָכֶיהָ דַרְכֵי־נֹעַם
> וְכָל־נְתִיבוֹתֶיהָ שָׁלוֹם:
>
> 18 עֵץ־חַיִּים הִיא לַמַּחֲזִיקִים בָּהּ
> וְתֹמְכֶיהָ מְאֻשָּׁר:

How does the order of the verses in the תַּנַ"ךְ differ from our version in the siddur?

_____

The two wooden rollers to which the Torah parchment is attached are also called עֲצֵי חַיִּים (the plural of עֵץ חַיִּים), trees of life.

Why is this an appropriate name for the rollers?

_____

In the following midrash, the Torah is compared to another object in nature—water.

> The Torah is like water. See how water comes down from heaven? Thus the Torah came down from heaven. See how water cleanses people? Thus the Torah cleanses the soul. See how rain water comes down in drops and forms rivers? Thus Torah is learned one bit at a time until the learner is like a flowing stream of knowledge…. Just as water is a source of life for the world, so the Torah is a source of life for the world.

(SHIR HASHIRIM RABBAH 1:19)

Choose one of the water metaphors that you find most interesting in the midrash and explain it.

_____

_____

_____

The rabbis who wrote this midrash lived in an agricultural society, where water was central to life. Think of something that is central in our lives and write a metaphor using it to describe the Torah.

See how _____

_____?

Thus the Torah _____

_____

chapter 7

Have you ever made a promise of loyalty to a friend? Perhaps you made a pact to stay friends forever or to defend one another. There are lots of ways to pledge loyalty. A bride and groom pledge their loyalty to each other during their wedding ceremony. Scouts promise to follow the principles of their organization. School children pledge allegiance to the flag of the United States of America.

עָלֵינוּ, a prayer that is recited near the end of the service, is a pledge of loyalty and a prayer of praise to God.

Practice reading עָלֵינוּ aloud.

1. עָלֵינוּ לְשַׁבֵּחַ לַאֲדוֹן הַכֹּל, לָתֵת גְּדֻלָּה לְיוֹצֵר בְּרֵאשִׁית,

2. שֶׁלֹּא עָשָׂנוּ כְּגוֹיֵי הָאֲרָצוֹת, וְלֹא שָׂמָנוּ כְּמִשְׁפְּחוֹת הָאֲדָמָה,

3. שֶׁלֹּא שָׂם חֶלְקֵנוּ כָּהֶם, וְגוֹרָלֵנוּ כְּכָל הֲמוֹנָם.

4. וַאֲנַחְנוּ כּוֹרְעִים וּמִשְׁתַּחֲוִים וּמוֹדִים,

5. לִפְנֵי מֶלֶךְ, מַלְכֵי הַמְּלָכִים, הַקָּדוֹשׁ בָּרוּךְ הוּא.

6. שֶׁהוּא נוֹטֶה שָׁמַיִם וְיוֹסֵד אָרֶץ, וּמוֹשַׁב יְקָרוֹ בַּשָּׁמַיִם מִמַּעַל,

7. וּשְׁכִינַת עֻזּוֹ בְּגָבְהֵי מְרוֹמִים.

8. הוּא אֱלֹהֵינוּ אֵין עוֹד. אֱמֶת מַלְכֵּנוּ, אֶפֶס זוּלָתוֹ,

9. כַּכָּתוּב בְּתוֹרָתוֹ: וְיָדַעְתָּ הַיּוֹם וַהֲשֵׁבֹתָ אֶל לְבָבֶךָ,

10. כִּי יְיָ הוּא הָאֱלֹהִים בַּשָּׁמַיִם מִמַּעַל וְעַל הָאָרֶץ מִתָּחַת, אֵין עוֹד.

11. וְנֶאֱמַר: וְהָיָה יְיָ לְמֶלֶךְ עַל כָּל הָאָרֶץ,

12. בַּיּוֹם הַהוּא יִהְיֶה יְיָ אֶחָד וּשְׁמוֹ אֶחָד.

1. It is our duty (it is upon us) to praise the God of all, to praise the Creator of the universe,

2. who has set us apart from other families of the earth,

3. giving us a unique destiny.

4. And we bend the knee, bow and give thanks,

5. before the Ruler of rulers, The Holy One who is blessed.

6. For God spread out the heavens and formed the earth, and resides in the heavens above;

7. and God's strengths rest in the heights.

8. God is our God, there is none else. In truth God alone is our Ruler,

9. as it is written in the Torah: Know this day and take it to heart,

10. for Adonai is the God in the heavens above and on the earth below. There is none else.

11. And it is said: Adonai will rule all the land.

12. On that day, Adonai will be One and God's name will be One.

Many of the words in עָלֵינוּ end with the suffix נוּ ("us" or "our"). Circle all the words in עָלֵינוּ ending with נוּ. How many words did you circle? _____

Praying together as a community can give us a feeling of belonging and a sense that we are not alone in our prayers.

Do you think it is important to pray as a community? Why or why not?

_____

_____

_____

_____

Create a Prayer Dictionary

Write the English words or phrases from the list below next to the matching Hebrew.

- IT IS OUR DUTY (IT IS UPON US) • TO PRAISE • TO (THE) CREATOR
- AND BOW • AND GIVE THANKS • ALL • AND WE • BEND THE KNEE

1. עָלֵינוּ _t(the) creator_

2. לְשַׁבֵּחַ _give thanks_

3. הַכֹּל _____

4. לְיוֹצֵר _____

5. וַאֲנַחְנוּ _____

6. כּוֹרְעִים _bend the knee_

7. וּמִשְׁתַּחֲוִים _____

8. וּמוֹדִים _____

Search and Circle

Circle the Hebrew word that means the same as the English.

1. to (the) creator	לָאָדוֹן	לְשַׁבֵּחַ	לְיוֹצֵר
2. give thanks	מוֹדִים	וַאֲנַחְנוּ	וּמִשְׁתַּחֲוִים
3. all	בָּחַר	הַכֹּל	עָלֵינוּ
4. and bow	מֶלֶךְ	וּמוֹדִים	וּמִשְׁתַּחֲוִים
5. to praise	עָלֵינוּ	לְיוֹצֵר	לְשַׁבֵּחַ
6. and we	וַאֲנַחְנוּ	עָלֵינוּ	וּמִשְׁתַּחֲוִים
7. it is our duty (it is upon us)	עוֹד	מִמַּעַל	עָלֵינוּ
8. bend the knee	(כּוֹרְעִים)	הָעַמִּים	יְהַלְלוּ

42

Prayer Background

עָלֵינוּ is one of our oldest prayers. It was written about 2,000 years ago. It was originally part of the Rosh Hashanah service, and around the 13th century it became part of the daily prayer service. עָלֵינוּ is so important that it was also recited by Jewish men and women who were condemned to death for refusing to convert to other religions. Those Jews defiantly sang out their belief in one God and their hope for a perfect world.

Today, in our country, we are allowed to practice our religion freely. What do *you* do that makes you feel Jewish?

I do tpd Jewishschool

Prayer Moves

When we recite עָלֵינוּ, we can physically act out the fourth line of the prayer. Based on the dictionary you created on page 42, translate the words below from the fourth line of the prayer.

וַאֲנַחְנוּ כּוֹרְעִים וּמִשְׁתַּחֲוִים וּמוֹדִים

We bend our knees at the word כּוֹרְעִים, bow slightly at the word וּמִשְׁתַּחֲוִים, and then stand upright at the word לְפְנֵי. In this way we act out the words of the prayer.

What is the name of another prayer in which we bow to God? _____
(Hint: It's also called the Standing Prayer.)

Why do you think we bow during these prayers? _____

Some congregations add the following line from Pirkei Avot to the service:

1. עַל שְׁלשָׁה דְבָרִים הָעוֹלָם עוֹמֵד:
עַל הַתּוֹרָה, וְעַל הָעֲבוֹדָה, וְעַל גְּמִילוּת חֲסָדִים.

   1. *Our world stands on three things:*
   on Torah, on worship, and on acts of loving-kindness. (PIRKEI AVOT 1:2)

Another quote from Pirkei Avot presents a different perspective. Read the selection.

2. עַל שְׁלשָׁה דְבָרִים הָעוֹלָם עוֹמֵד:
עַל הַדִּין, וְעַל הָאֱמֶת, וְעַל הַשָּׁלוֹם...

   2. *Our world stands on three things:*
   on justice, on truth, and on peace. (PIRKEI AVOT 1:18)

Each quote presents a vision of how we can work to perfect the world and make it a better place.

According to each of the teachings, how can we make the world a better place?

Pirkei Avot Quote 1

Acts of Lovingkindness

Pirkei Avot Quote 2

Peace

Which teaching would you rather follow? Why?

Pirkei Avot Quote 2

אֲדוֹן עוֹלָם

אֲדוֹן עוֹלָם ("Sovereign of the World") is a concluding *piyyut* (poetic prayer) in the Shabbat morning service. The author is unknown, but the style suggests it originated in Spain in the 12th or 13th century. This *piyyut* declares that God is eternal, without a beginning or an end. The poet's spirit when sleeping is entrusted to God. Because of this last statement, some people say אֲדוֹן עוֹלָם before going to sleep at night.

Practice reading אֲדוֹן עוֹלָם aloud.

בְּטֶרֶם כָּל יְצִיר נִבְרָא.	1. אֲדוֹן עוֹלָם אֲשֶׁר מָלַךְ,
אֲזַי מֶלֶךְ שְׁמוֹ נִקְרָא.	2. לְעֵת נַעֲשָׂה בְחֶפְצוֹ כֹּל,
לְבַדּוֹ יִמְלֹךְ נוֹרָא.	3. וְאַחֲרֵי כִּכְלוֹת הַכֹּל,
וְהוּא יִהְיֶה בְּתִפְאָרָה.	4. וְהוּא הָיָה וְהוּא הֹוֶה,
לְהַמְשִׁיל לוֹ לְהַחְבִּירָה.	5. וְהוּא אֶחָד וְאֵין שֵׁנִי,
וְלוֹ הָעֹז וְהַמִּשְׂרָה.	6. בְּלִי רֵאשִׁית בְּלִי תַכְלִית,
וְצוּר חֶבְלִי בְּעֵת צָרָה.	7. וְהוּא אֵלִי וְחַי גּוֹאֲלִי,
מְנָת כּוֹסִי בְּיוֹם אֶקְרָא.	8. וְהוּא נִסִּי וּמָנוֹס לִי,
בְּעֵת אִישַׁן וְאָעִירָה.	9. בְּיָדוֹ אַפְקִיד רוּחִי,
יְיָ לִי וְלֹא אִירָא.	10. וְעִם רוּחִי גְּוִיָּתִי,

There are lots of tunes for אֲדוֹן עוֹלָם. Some are fast and merry; others are slow and somber. Do you think the words of אֲדוֹן עוֹלָם fit one type of melody more than another?

Explain your answer.

_____

_____

45

קַדִּישׁ

chapter 8

Near the end of the service, we say a prayer in memory of those who have died. Surprisingly, this prayer, the קַדִּישׁ, doesn't once mention death. Instead, it praises God, speaks of God's holiness, and expresses our wish for peace on earth.

Practice reading the קַדִּישׁ aloud.

1. יִתְגַּדַּל וְיִתְקַדַּשׁ שְׁמֵהּ רַבָּא

2. בְּעָלְמָא דִּי בְרָא כִרְעוּתֵהּ, וְיַמְלִיךְ מַלְכוּתֵהּ

3. בְּחַיֵּיכוֹן וּבְיוֹמֵיכוֹן וּבְחַיֵּי דְכָל בֵּית יִשְׂרָאֵל,

4. בַּעֲגָלָא וּבִזְמַן קָרִיב, וְאִמְרוּ אָמֵן.

5. יְהֵא שְׁמֵהּ רַבָּא מְבָרַךְ לְעָלַם וּלְעָלְמֵי עָלְמַיָּא.

6. יִתְבָּרַךְ וְיִשְׁתַּבַּח וְיִתְפָּאַר וְיִתְרוֹמַם וְיִתְנַשֵּׂא

7. וְיִתְהַדָּר וְיִתְעַלֶּה וְיִתְהַלָּל שְׁמֵהּ דְּקֻדְשָׁא, בְּרִיךְ הוּא.

8. לְעֵלָּא מִן כָּל בִּרְכָתָא וְשִׁירָתָא, תֻּשְׁבְּחָתָא וְנֶחֱמָתָא,

9. דַּאֲמִירָן בְּעָלְמָא, וְאִמְרוּ אָמֵן.

10. יְהֵא שְׁלָמָא רַבָּא מִן שְׁמַיָּא וְחַיִּים עָלֵינוּ וְעַל כָּל יִשְׂרָאֵל, וְאִמְרוּ אָמֵן.

11. עוֹשֶׂה שָׁלוֹם בִּמְרוֹמָיו הוּא יַעֲשֶׂה שָׁלוֹם עָלֵינוּ וְעַל כָּל יִשְׂרָאֵל, וְאִמְרוּ אָמֵן.

1. *May God's name be great and may it be made holy*
2. *in the world created according to God's will. And may God rule*
3. *in our own lives and in our own days, and in the life of all the house of Israel,*
4. *swiftly and soon, and say, Amen.*
5. *May God's great name be blessed forever and ever.*
6. *Blessed, praised, glorified, exalted, extolled,*
7. *honored, magnified, and adored be the name of the Holy One, blessed is God;*

8. *though God is beyond all the blessings, songs, adorations, and consolations*

9. *that are spoken in the world, and say, Amen.*

10. *May there be great peace from heaven and life for us and for all of Israel, and say, Amen.*

11. *May God who makes peace in the heaven, make peace for us and for all of Israel. And say, Amen.*

Read the last two lines of the English translation of the קַדִּישׁ **again. What do we wish for in these lines?** _____

Why do you think the קַדִּישׁ **ends with this wish?**

_____

_____

The Hebrew-Aramaic Connection

Do you notice something different about the language of the קַדִּישׁ? Most of the words are in Aramaic. Aramaic is a language similar to Hebrew that was spoken by the Jews at the time of Ezra the prophet in the 5th century B.C.E. and for the next thousand years.

The words in the קַדִּישׁ may look difficult, but in fact, you already know many of them!

In the right-hand column below are Hebrew prayer words you have learned. In the left-hand column are related words from the קַדִּישׁ.

Draw a line from each Hebrew word to the related Aramaic word.

יִתְגַּדֵּל	קָדוֹשׁ .1
וְיִתְקַדַּשׁ	בָּרוּךְ .2
בְּעָלְמָא	יִמְלֹךְ .3
וְיַמְלִיךְ	הַגָּדוֹל .4
בְּרִיךְ	שָׁמַיִם .5
שְׁלָמָא	שָׁלוֹם .6
שְׁמַיָּא	הָעוֹלָם .7

Create a Prayer Dictionary

Write the English words or phrases from the list below next to the matching Aramaic.

- BLESSED - HEAVEN - IN THE WORLD - AND MAY (GOD) RULE
- MAY (GOD'S NAME) BE GREAT - BLESSINGS - PEACE
- AND MAY (GOD'S NAME) BE HOLY

_____	בְּרִיךְ .5	*may (God's name) be great*	יִתְגַּדַּל .1
_____	בִּרְכָתָא .6	_____	וְיִתְקַדַּשׁ .2
_____	שְׁלָמָא .7	_____	בְּעָלְמָא .3
_____	שְׁמַיָּא .8	_____	וְיַמְלִיךְ .4

Did You Know?

There are other versions of the קַדִּישׁ too; for example, the חֲצִי קַדִּישׁ ("half Kaddish"). The קַדִּישׁ divides up the service, almost the way a file divider separates the subjects in your school binder. It indicates the end of one section of the service and the beginning of the next.

Idm ...
Dawe

48

Root Search

The numbered words below are found in the קַדִּישׁ. Above them is a list of their roots. Write the root for each word. *Note: You may have to use the same root twice.*

> מלכ   קדש   שלמ   ברכ   גדל

5. שְׁלָמָא _____ _____   1. יִתְגַּדַּל _____ _____

6. מַלְכוּתֵהּ _____ _____   2. וְיִתְקַדַּשׁ _____ _____

7. בְּרִיךְ _____ _____   3. וְיַמְלִיךְ _____ _____

8. קַדִּישׁ _____ _____   4. בִּרְכָתָא _____ _____

Did You Know?

We are not sure who wrote the קַדִּישׁ or when. It probably developed over hundreds of years. We do know that it became a prayer for mourners about 800 years ago.

In some congregations, only the people reciting the Mourner's Kaddish—those in mourning or observing *yahrzeit*, the anniversary of a loved one's death—stand as they recite the קַדִּישׁ. In other congregations, everyone stands as a sign of support for the mourners or to remember those who died in the Holocaust. Sometimes all congregants recite the prayer together.

In most congregations, the קַדִּישׁ is only recited in the presence of a מִנְיָן, ten Jewish adults. The entire congregation joins in to recite the line below.

יְהֵא שְׁמֵהּ רַבָּא מְבָרַךְ לְעָלַם וּלְעָלְמֵי עָלְמַיָּא.

May God's great name be blessed forever and ever.

What atmosphere does it help create when the entire congregation joins in?

_____

_____

Back to the Sources

Both the קַדִּישׁ and the עֲמִידָה end with the same prayer for peace:

עוֹשֶׂה שָׁלוֹם בִּמְרוֹמָיו הוּא יַעֲשֶׂה שָׁלוֹם עָלֵינוּ וְעַל כָּל יִשְׂרָאֵל,
וְאִמְרוּ אָמֵן.

May God who makes peace in the heavens make peace for us and for all of Israel.
And say, Amen.

Read the following midrash about making peace, then answer the questions that follow.

When the sun and the moon were created they began to argue. The sun said, "I will rule the day," to which the moon replied, "No, it is I who will rule the day!" They came before God. The sun said, "I wish to rule the day," and the moon, "No, I wish to rule the day." God called to the sun and said, "You will rule the day" and to the moon God said, "You will rule the night." And so it is written in the Torah: And God called the light day, and the darkness God called night (Genesis 1:5). To compensate for the moon's sacrifice, God gave the moon the stars as escorts in the night.

Why do you think the sun and the moon could not solve the controversy on their own and needed God's arbitration?

_____

_____

What can we learn from this midrash about making peace?

_____

_____

Describe an incident in your own life when you needed a mediator. What happened? How was the situation resolved?

_____

_____

50

Prayer Moves

Just as in the עֲמִידָה, when we come to עֹשֶׂה שָׁלוֹם at the end of the קַדִּיש, many congregations do the following:

1. Take three steps back.
2. Bow from the waist to the left and say עֹשֶׂה שָׁלוֹם בִּמְרוֹמָיו.
3. Bow from the waist to the right and say הוּא יַעֲשֶׂה שָׁלוֹם עָלֵינוּ.
4. Bow forward and say וְעַל כָּל יִשְׂרָאֵל וְאִמְרוּ אָמֵן.
5. Return to our original position.

Prayer Connections

You may recall a paragraph in the haggadah in which we read about the "bread of affliction" and invite all who are needy to celebrate Passover with us. The entire paragraph, הָא לַחְמָא עַנְיָא, is written in Aramaic, the language of the קַדִּיש.

Can you read הָא לַחְמָא עַנְיָא? It's hard to do!

1. הָא לַחְמָא עַנְיָא דִי אֲכָלוּ אַבָהָתָנָא בְּאַרְעָא דְמִצְרָיִם.

2. כָּל דִכְפִין יֵיתֵי וְיֵכָל, כָּל דִצְרִיךְ יֵיתֵי וְיִפְסַח.

3. הָשַׁתָּא הָכָא, לַשָׁנָה הַבָּאָה בְּאַרְעָא דְיִשְׂרָאֵל.

4. הָשַׁתָּא עַבְדֵי, לַשָׁנָה הַבָּאָה בְּנֵי חוֹרִין.

1. *This is the bread of affliction which our ancestors ate in the land of Egypt.*
2. *Let all who are hungry come and eat. Let all who are needy come and celebrate Passover.*
3. *At present we are here; next year may we be in Israel.*
4. *At present we are slaves; next year may we be free people.*

Complete the following activities:
1. What is another name for "bread of affliction"? _____
2. Find and circle the word for "Israel" in the Aramaic passage.
3. Underline the Aramaic equivalent of לֶחֶם, the Hebrew word for "bread."
4. What does this passage teach us about how to behave towards other people?

chapter 9

אֵין כֵּאלֹהֵינוּ

At the end of the service, we often sing a final hymn of praise, אֵין כֵּאלֹהֵינוּ, an upbeat, rhythmic song that honors God in four ways—as our God, our Sovereign, our Ruler, and our Savior.

Practice reading אֵין כֵּאלֹהֵינוּ aloud.

1. אֵין כֵּאלֹהֵינוּ,	אֵין כַּאדוֹנֵינוּ,
2. אֵין כְּמַלְכֵּנוּ,	אֵין כְּמוֹשִׁיעֵנוּ.
3. מִי כֵאלֹהֵינוּ,	מִי כַאדוֹנֵינוּ,
4. מִי כְמַלְכֵּנוּ,	מִי כְמוֹשִׁיעֵנוּ.
5. נוֹדֶה לֵאלֹהֵינוּ,	נוֹדֶה לַאדוֹנֵינוּ,
6. נוֹדֶה לְמַלְכֵּנוּ,	נוֹדֶה לְמוֹשִׁיעֵנוּ.
7. בָּרוּךְ אֱלֹהֵינוּ,	בָּרוּךְ אֲדוֹנֵינוּ,
8. בָּרוּךְ מַלְכֵּנוּ,	בָּרוּךְ מוֹשִׁיעֵנוּ.
9. אַתָּה הוּא אֱלֹהֵינוּ,	אַתָּה הוּא אֲדוֹנֵינוּ,
10. אַתָּה הוּא מַלְכֵּנוּ,	אַתָּה הוּא מוֹשִׁיעֵנוּ.

1. There is none like our God, There is none like our Sovereign,
2. There is none like our Ruler, There is none like our Savior.
3. Who is like our God? Who is like our Sovereign?
4. Who is like our Ruler? Who is like our Savior?
5. We will give thanks to our God, We will give thanks to our Sovereign,
6. We will give thanks to our Ruler, We will give thanks to our Savior.
7. Blessed is our God, Blessed is our Sovereign,
8. Blessed is our Ruler, Blessed is our Savior.
9. You are our God, You are our Sovereign,
10. You are our Ruler, You are our Savior.

Create a Prayer Dictionary

Write the English words or phrases from the list below next to the matching Hebrew.

• YOU • LIKE OUR SAVIOR • LIKE OUR SOVEREIGN • LIKE OUR GOD
• LIKE OUR RULER • WHO IS • WE WILL GIVE THANKS • BLESSED
• THERE IS NONE

6. מִי _____

1. אֵין _____

7. נוֹדֶה _____

2. כֵּאלֹהֵינוּ _like our God_

8. בָּרוּךְ _____

3. כַּאדוֹנֵינוּ _like our Sovereign_

9. אַתָּה _____

4. כְּמַלְכֵּנוּ _____

5. כְּמוֹשִׁיעֵנוּ _____

A Hymn of Praise

אֵין כֵּאלֹהֵינוּ was written before the 9th century C.E. That makes it over 1,000 years old! It is an important statement of our belief in God.

Reread the English translation of אֵין כֵּאלֹהֵינוּ on page 52.

In your own words, describe the belief in God that we express in אֵין כֵּאלֹהֵינוּ.

_____

_____

_____

Prayer Arithmetic

The following pairs of equations will help you discover two basic rules in Hebrew grammar. For the first pair, read both sets of words. Subtract the words on the second line from the words on the first and write your answer on the blank below. Repeat with the second pair of equations. The pair in each equation should have the same solution.

like our Ruler	=	כְּמַלְכֵּנוּ	**1**	like our Sovereign	=	כַּאדוֹנֵינוּ
– our Ruler	=	מַלְכֵּנוּ		– our Sovereign	=	אֲדוֹנֵינוּ

_____

_____ = כְּ   _____ = כַּ

our God	=	אֱלֹהֵינוּ	**2**	our Savior	=	מוֹשִׁיעֵנוּ
– God (of)	=	אֱלֹהֵי		– Savior	=	מוֹשִׁיעַ

_____

_____ = נוּ   _____ = נוּ

1. **What do the prefixes כְּ and כַּ mean?** _____

2. **What does the suffix נוּ mean?** _____

Turn back to the prayer on page 52.

Circle all the כְּ prefixes. How many did you circle? _____

Underline all the נוּ suffixes. How many did you underline? _____

Why do you think this prayer was written in the plural, using "us" and "our" instead of "my"?

_____

_____

_____

Putting It Together

You know the beginning and the ending of each word below.

Write the number of the matching English meaning above each Hebrew word.

1. like our Ruler

2. like our Savior

3. like our Sovereign

4. like our God

Now circle the main part (not the prefix or suffix) of each Hebrew word above. The first one has been done for you.

Each of these main parts is actually a name for God. You may not recognize the names for God at first, because when a word has a prefix or suffix added, it may change its vowels or lose a final letter.

Connect the names for God in the first column to the related words from אֵין כֵּאלֹהֵינוּ **in the second column.**

2	1
אֱלֹהֵינוּ	מֶלֶךְ
מַלְכֵּנוּ	אָדוֹן
אֲדוֹנֵינוּ	מוֹשִׁיעַ
מוֹשִׁיעֵנוּ	אֱלֹהִים

Architecture of the Prayer

See how carefully structured אֵין כֵּאלֹהֵינוּ is. Read the first three stanzas of the prayer again, then complete the activities that follow.

אֵין כַּאדוֹנֵינוּ,	1. אֵין כֵּאלֹהֵינוּ,
אֵין כְּמוֹשִׁיעֵנוּ.	2. אֵין כְּמַלְכֵּנוּ,
מִי כַאדוֹנֵינוּ,	3. מִי כֵאלֹהֵינוּ,
מִי כְמוֹשִׁיעֵנוּ.	4. מִי כְמַלְכֵּנוּ,
נוֹדֶה לַאדוֹנֵינוּ,	5. נוֹדֶה לֵאלֹהֵינוּ,
נוֹדֶה לְמוֹשִׁיעֵנוּ.	6. נוֹדֶה לְמַלְכֵּנוּ,

1. Circle the Hebrew word for "there is none" the first time it appears. Write the word here. _____

2. Underline the Hebrew word for "who is?" the first time it appears. Write the word here. _____

3. Put a box around the Hebrew word for "we will give thanks" the first time it appears. Write the word here. _____

In the spaces below, write the initial letters of the three words you wrote to spell out a new, "secret" word. *Remember:* ב *at the end of a word is written* ן.

_____ _____ _____

When do we say this word? _____

Bonus question:

Why do you think this acrostic comes at this point in the service? (*Hint: Think about where* אֵין כֵּאלֹהֵינוּ *is located in the service.*)

_____

Read the following midrash about honoring and praising God. Then answer the questions that follow.

Once when Hillel had finished teaching his students, he walked towards home with them. "Rabbi," they asked, "where are you going?" "To perform a mitzvah," he answered. "What mitzvah is it?" "To bathe in the bathhouse." "Is that really a mitzvah?" they asked in surprise. He replied, "If someone is appointed to scrape and clean the statues of the Roman Emperor that stand in the theaters and streets, is paid for the work, and is even associated with the nobility, how much more should I, who am created in God's image, take care of my body!"

How does Hillel honor God in this midrash?

_____

_____

Do you think this is a good way to honor God? Explain your answer.

_____

_____

_____

Give three other examples of ways you can honor God by your actions.

1. _____

2. _____

3. _____

We're approaching the end of our book. You have learned many prayers in the Torah service and the concluding part of the Shabbat morning service. Let's review.

Putting Things in Order

The Torah service has three parts: (1) taking the Torah out of the Ark, (2) reading from the Torah, and (3) returning the Torah to the Ark.

In the right-hand column below are the names of prayers in the Torah service. In the left-hand column are short descriptions of the prayers.

Draw a line between each prayer and its matching description.

The blessings before and after the Torah reading	1. לְךָ יְיָ הַגְּדֻלָה
Sung by the community as the Torah is taken out of the Ark and paraded around the congregation	2. מִזְמוֹר לְדָוִד: הָבוּ לַיָי בְּנֵי אֵלִים
The blessings before and after the haftarah reading	3. וְזֹאת הַתּוֹרָה אֲשֶׁר שָׂם מֹשֶׁה
"It is a tree of life," sung as we return the Torah to the Ark	4. בִּרְכוֹת הַתּוֹרָה
Sung by the congregation as the Torah is lifted	5. אֵין כָּמוֹךָ/אַב הָרַחֲמִים
Sung during the procession returning the Torah to the Ark	6. עֵץ חַיִּים הִיא
A prayer praising God at the beginning of the Torah service	7. בִּרְכוֹת הַהַפְטָרָה

Name That Prayer

Below are the names of five prayers you have learned. Write the name of each prayer above the lines selected from that prayer. Then read each selection aloud.

בִּרְכוֹת הַתּוֹרָה   קַדִּישׁ   עָלֵינוּ   אֵין כֵּאלֹהֵינוּ   בִּרְכוֹת הַהַפְטָרָה

1. _____

וַאֲנַחְנוּ כּוֹרְעִים וּמִשְׁתַּחֲוִים וּמוֹדִים,

לִפְנֵי מֶלֶךְ, מַלְכֵי הַמְּלָכִים, הַקָּדוֹשׁ בָּרוּךְ הוּא.

2. _____

מִי כֵאלֹהֵינוּ, מִי כַאדוֹנֵינוּ, מִי כְמַלְכֵּנוּ, מִי כְמוֹשִׁיעֵנוּ.

3. _____

אֲשֶׁר בָּחַר בִּנְבִיאִים טוֹבִים,

וְרָצָה בְדִבְרֵיהֶם הַנֶּאֱמָרִים בֶּאֱמֶת.

4. _____

יִתְבָּרַךְ וְיִשְׁתַּבַּח וְיִתְפָּאַר וְיִתְרוֹמַם וְיִתְנַשֵּׂא

וְיִתְהַדָּר וְיִתְעַלֶּה וְיִתְהַלָּל שְׁמֵהּ דְקֻדְשָׁא, בְּרִיךְ הוּא.

5. _____

אֲשֶׁר בָּחַר בָּנוּ מִכָּל הָעַמִּים

וְנָתַן לָנוּ אֶת תּוֹרָתוֹ.

בָּרוּךְ אַתָּה, יְיָ, נוֹתֵן הַתּוֹרָה.

True or False

Read each statement below. Put a ✔ if the statement is true and an ✗ if it is false.

1. In most congregations, the קַדִּישׁ can only be recited in the
   presence of a minyan. _____

2. We bow during עָלֵינוּ. _____

3. The Torah reader is always the same person who recites the
   Torah blessings. _____

4. When the Torah is lifted the congregation sings אֵין כֵּאלֹהֵינוּ. _____

5. The haftarah blessings praise the prophets of truth and righteousness. _____

6. We read the Torah from a scroll and the haftarah from a printed book. _____

7. We remain seated when the Ark is opened. _____

8. The Torah is the first part of the Bible; the Book of Prophets is the
   second; and Writings, which includes psalms and proverbs, is third. _____

Memory Challenge

The verses of אֵין כֵּאלֹהֵינוּ are out of order below.
Number the verses in the correct order of the prayer. The first one has been done for
you. Then read the prayer in the correct order.

בָּרוּךְ אֱלֹהֵינוּ,	בָּרוּךְ אֲדוֹנֵינוּ,	◯
בָּרוּךְ מַלְכֵּנוּ,	בָּרוּךְ מוֹשִׁיעֵנוּ.	
אֵין כֵּאלֹהֵינוּ,	אֵין כַּאדוֹנֵינוּ,	①
אֵין כְּמַלְכֵּנוּ,	אֵין כְּמוֹשִׁיעֵנוּ.	
מִי כֵאלֹהֵינוּ,	מִי כַאדוֹנֵינוּ,	◯
מִי כְמַלְכֵּנוּ,	מִי כְמוֹשִׁיעֵנוּ.	
אַתָּה הוּא אֱלֹהֵינוּ,	אַתָּה הוּא אֲדוֹנֵינוּ,	◯
אַתָּה הוּא מַלְכֵּנוּ,	אַתָּה הוּא מוֹשִׁיעֵנוּ.	
נוֹדֶה לֵאלֹהֵינוּ,	נוֹדֶה לַאדוֹנֵינוּ,	◯
נוֹדֶה לְמַלְכֵּנוּ,	נוֹדֶה לְמוֹשִׁיעֵנוּ.	

Word Search

Below are sixteen key prayer words that you learned in this book. For each word, find the English meaning in the Word Search and circle it. The English words appear from left to right, top to bottom, bottom to top, or on a diagonal. Some letters may appear in more than one word.

13. מוֹדִים   9. צֶדֶק   5. בָּחַר   1. מַלְכוּת

14. אֲנַחְנוּ   10. טוֹבִים   6. נָתַן   2. רַחֲמִים

15. שָׁלוֹם   11. דָּוִד   7. שֵׁם   3. יְרוּשָׁלַיִם

16. קָדוֹשׁ   12. קוֹל   8. עַם   4. צִיּוֹן

J	U	S	T	I	C	E	P	E	A	C	E
D	A	V	I	D	M	Z	N	Y	I	S	M
S	O	V	E	R	E	I	G	N	T	Y	S
E	L	O	S	M	R	O	N	A	O	L	R
F	G	O	O	D	C	N	O	M	V	O	W
H	O	L	H	N	Y	Z	I	E	W	E	Y
V	O	I	C	E	F	L	T	Q	B	L	L
G	U	J	E	R	U	S	A	L	E	M	O
P	E	N	R	T	H	A	N	K	H	T	H

By establishing a weekly Torah service, the rabbis wanted to ensure that the Jewish people would regularly study the Torah. When you listen to the Torah and haftarah readings, you too are following the rabbis' plan!

Read the following midrash about the Torah.

Rabbi Meir said: When the Israelites stood before Mount Sinai to receive the Torah, God said to them, "I am giving you the Torah; bring me good guarantors (people who will vouch for you) that you will keep it, and I will give it to you." The Israelites replied, "Our ancestors are our guarantors." God said, "Your ancestors need guarantors themselves! Bring me good guarantors that you will keep the Torah, and I will give it to you." The Israelites replied, "Our prophets are our guarantors." God said, "They too are not free of sin." The Israelites said, "Our children are our guarantors." God said, "They are indeed good guarantors. Only because of your children will I give you the Torah."

Why do you think God needed guarantors before giving the Torah to the Israelites?

_____

What, in your opinion, makes the children good guarantors?

_____

_____

You are one of those guarantors. What can you do to ensure that the Torah is preserved? What can we do as a community?

_____

_____

_____

Conclusion

In this book you have learned the prayers in the Torah service and the concluding prayers in the Shabbat morning service. Many are prayers praising God—for giving us the Torah, for giving us the prophets and their teachings, or for working wonders in the world. Some include the wish for peace. One pledges loyalty to God.

As you prepare for your Bar or Bat Mitzvah, write your own prayer. It can be personal (thanking God for something you have) or general (a wish for the community or the Jewish people). Feel free to use some of the themes you have studied, or integrate other feelings or thoughts you find meaningful or powerful.

_____

_____

_____

_____

_____

_____

חֲזַק חֲזַק וְנִתְחַזֵּק.

May you go from strength to strength.